★ ★ ★ ★ ★ ★ ★ ★ ★ ★ ★ ★ ★ ★

NITRO CIRCUS

BEST OF SCOOTER

RIPLEY
PUBLISHING

a Jim Pattison Company

EXTREME FREESTYLE SCOOTERING IS HERE TO STAY

TRICKS, AIR, FLIPS, WHIPS: RIDERS DO IT ALL!

Freestyle scootering, also known as simply *riding*, was born almost 20 years ago and has gained traction in skate parks around the world over the past 10 years. It is an action sport that's a marriage of skateboarding and BMX freestyle. The riders perform freestyle tricks or stunts on specially designed, professional kick scooters.

It's not part of the X Games (yet!), but dedicated riders are participating in competitions such as Nitro World Games, the ISA World Championships, and others. As the sport's popularity soars, scooter riders like Ryan Williams of Australia are increasingly getting sponsorships and turning pro. This sport is growing rapidly in popularity around the world!

KEY FACTS

Scootering has its own governing bodies and national teams in the UK, Australia, and America.

★★★★★★★★★★★

Many accomplished scooter riders make the jump from BMX and skateboarding with great success.

★★★★★★★★★★★

Don't try these amazing tricks with a toy scooter. You need the specialty kind!

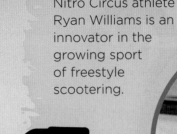

Nitro Circus athlete Ryan Williams is an innovator in the growing sport of freestyle scootering.

Scooters allow riders to do tricks inspired by both BMX and skate, including tailwhips, barspins, frontflips, backflips, barspins, grinds, and more.

Professional-grade scooters have many advantages over toy scooters that make them suitable for cool tricks, including sturdier decks and threadless forks.

Dakota Schuetz has a Guinness World Record for performing 15 backflips in one minute on his scooter.

THE COMPETITION IS HEATING UP

CAN YOU SEND IT?

As pro scooter riders get more sponsorships and the sport becomes more popular, there are more competitions and championships where riders can show their stuff, gain recognition, and prove that this extreme sport is just as exciting, dangerous, and difficult as its predecessors!

Nitro World Games and the ISA (International Scooter Association) World Championships are two serious venues for scooter riders to show their tricks and take home the gold. Nitro World Games has a Scooter Best Trick event and is continually adding more scooter-related events to their schedule, and the ISA World Championships boasts riders from all over the world competing for the venerable title of World Scooter Champion!

Jordan Clark, from Chichester Harbour, England, began riding in 2011. He was crowned World Scooter Champion in 2015, 2016, and 2018!

The Scooter Best Trick event at Nitro World Games is a crowd favorite!

NITRO WORLD GAMES
MAKING AND BREAKING WORLD RECORDS!

First held in 2016 and created by Nitro Circus, Nitro World Games is an international action sports competition that attracts the best athletes from around the world.

Athletes in BMX, FMX (freestyle motocross), scootering, rallycross, and skateboarding compete for medals. In just a few years, these games have seen many broken records and world firsts!

SCOOTFEST: A CELEBRATION OF SCOOTERING

THE LARGEST SCOOTER EVENT IN THE WORLD!

ScootFest is an annual competition that showcases the sport of freestyle scootering in the UK. It takes place in Corby, England, over a weekend and features scooter competitions for amateurs and professionals in the three areas of Park, Bowl, and Street.

Along with the World Cup Team event, which crowns the best team, ScootFest also includes King of Bowl, King of Park, and King of Street events, which are invitation-only. Riders with the highest points in each area win, and the highest point earner is crowned the wildly coveted King of Kings winner.

If that's not enough, the legendary ScootFest Am Jam is also a fan favorite. It's where up-and-coming amateurs and first-timers compete in a friendly jam-session competition. And that's not all! ScootFest also hosts the Scoot GB (Great Britain) Finals, including the British Championships (also called the Battle of Britain). You can see why ScootFest is described by some as two days of absolute mayhem!

SCOOTFEST AND THE KING OF KINGS EVENT

THE BEST OF THE BEST!

At ScootFest 2018, Richard Zelinka took first place in the King of Bowl competition, second place in Street, and eighth place in Park. This meant he won the prestigious King of Kings competition! It was his second year in a row to win the King of Kings crown—pretty impressive for this 19-year-old called a "scooter wunderkind" by many.

After the riders spend two full days laying down tricks on their scooters, the ultimate freestyle scooter athlete is crowned! ScootFest pairs with Nitro World Games to present this wildly popular King of Kings prize.

The King of Kings rewards the best overall rider who can trick it best on all three venues. Riders don't have to place first in each area to win King of Kings; they just have to place high enough in each to earn the most points overall. It's considered an acknowledgment of the best all-around freestyle scooter athlete in the world!

STREET

Scooters have been around for more than 100 years, but with the recent popularity and progression of the sport, two main styles of scooters (and scooter riding) have emerged: street and park.

Although street and park scooters have evolved for different styles of riding, both types of scooters can work for all tricks.

DID YOU KNOW?

Street riding is all about performing technical tricks with style. These scooters are typically larger and stronger than park scooters, with less focus on being lightweight and more focus on being grindable!

BAR GRIPS

Grips provide comfort for your hands and prevent slipping while riding.

HANDLEBARS

Street scooter handlebars are built for comfort over agility and so are bigger and heavier than park handlebars.

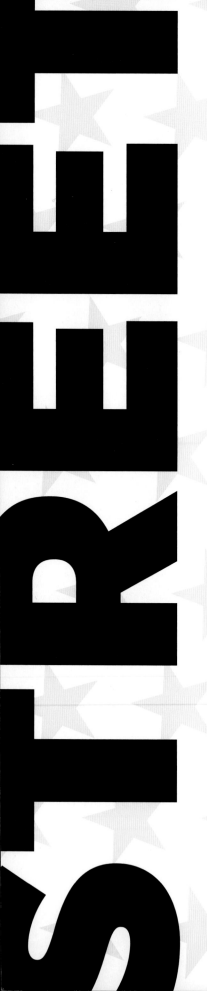

DECK

Longer, wider, and stronger decks give more foot space for comfort and more surface area for grinds.

WHEELS

Beginner scooters typically use plastic cores, but most higher-end scooters use a metal core to make them stronger and more durable.

PARK

Park style riding is all about doing as many tricks and combos as possible. This means that park scooters are made to be light and agile, perfect for tailwhips, briflips, scooter flips... and big air combos!

BAR GRIPS

A good grip is key for all scooter tricks, especially for tailwhips and barspins.

HANDLEBAR

Park scooters have shorter and more lightweight handlebars compared to street scooters. This makes them more agile and easier to move around in the air.

KEY FACTS

Scooters are sometimes referred to as "kick scooters" because you kick off the ground with your foot to propel the scooter forward. This "kick" is the difference from electric and gas-powered scooters.

Like many scooter tricks, styles of scooter riding come from the worlds of BMX and skateboarding!

FORKS

The top pros ride threadless forks. These provide more strength and allow for more precision riding around the skatepark.

DECK

Park scooters have shorter and lighter decks than street scooters.

PRO TIPS

Just because these are called "park scooters" doesn't mean they can't be ridden on the streets. Pick the scooter that fits your riding style, and just have fun shredding.

NITRO CIRCUS
RYAN WILLIAMS

WHEELS

Bigger wheels allow for more speed, which is needed to get more air and allow for bigger tricks and more combos.

RIDE SAFE AND SMART!
YOUR EQUIPMENT IS KEY!

When you're learning these sick scooter tricks, it's not "if" but "when" you will fall. But if you have the right protective gear, those falls won't faze you.

Protective gear will mean you can try more aggressive tricks, feel safer while learning, keep going after a fall, and build your skills faster! Don't expect to fly through the air without some safety gear!

DID YOU KNOW?

Top pro riders always practice with safety gear. They know if they get hurt, they might not be able to compete! Most competitions require riders to wear helmets.

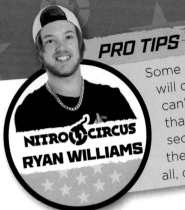

PRO TIPS

NITRO CIRCUS
RYAN WILLIAMS

Some skate parks and online organizations will donate proper helmets to riders if they can't afford them. Find an organization that will help you out. Also try looking in second-hand sports stores, but make sure the helmet hasn't been damaged. Most of all, don't use a regular bike helmet!

Pick a strong, sturdy "skate" style helmet that has more protection for the back of the head. If you can push the helmet inward using both hands, it's not strong enough. Bell Helmets are worn by most of the Nitro Circus athletes.

Gloves prevent callouses from the grips and protect your hands from cement and asphalt when you fall. When you're not in constant pain, you'll have more fun.

Your elbows and knees are often the first things that hit the ground when a trick goes wrong. Protect them so you can be up and riding in no time!

BUNNY HOP

TRICK #1

The bunny hop is when you jump straight up with two feet on the deck, then pull the scooter straight up as well.

Both wheels come off the ground at the same time. This trick is the foundation for all air tricks that follow!

NITRO METER

BEGINNER · INTERMEDIATE · ADVANCED · CRAZY!

NITRO CIRCUS
RYAN WILLIAMS

PRO TIPS

The bunny hop is a good place to start your scooter skills. It is the foundation of lots of tricks, so mastering the bunny hop is key to becoming a better scooter rider.

THE MANUAL

The manual is a great introduction to learning how to control and balance on your scooter. Riding on flat ground, pull the front wheel of the scooter off the ground, shifting all of your weight over the back wheel. It can help to keep your arms straight and your back foot over the brake to help with control.

The manual is all about finding the perfect balance point so that your front wheel isn't too high off the ground or too low! Tapping the brake will slow down your speed and bring the front wheel back to the ground.

NITRO METER
BEGINNER INTERMEDIATE ADVANCED CRAZY!

START WITH TH[E B]ASICS
STUNT SCOOTER SKILLS: BUILDING A FOUNDATION

With scootering, there are a few basic skills that are fundamental to learning everything else, no matter how difficult the combo!

You have to start by mastering these important and fundamental techniques, as they are the building blocks that you need to become a master at scootering!

BARSPIN

TRICK #3

Add a 360-degree barspin (spinning the handlebars around) while you're doing a hop to advance your skills and control.

NITRO METER

BEGINNER · INTERMEDIATE · ADVANCED · CRAZY!

NITRO CIRCUS
RYAN WILLIAMS

PRO TIPS

If you want to fly through the air with grace and ease, you have to start by mastering the fundamentals!

GRIND AN EDGE

Your newly mastered bunny hop will allow you to pop up onto ledges and rails to start grinding, which takes a lot of balance.

Grinds can be done using pegs or along the bottom of the scooter.

BEGINNER INTERMEDIATE ADVANCED CRAZY!

NITRO METER

MASTERING TH𝐄 MOV𝐄S!

STUNT SCOOTER SKILLS: NEXT STEPS

BAR

TRICK #5

TWIST

The bar twist is a nice add-on to any jump or run, and you can practice and even master it while standing firmly on the ground.

The bar twist can be done on both sides of your body, but it's best to start learning on your dominant side (usually right-hand side). Throw the bars back to your side, letting go with your non-dominant hand, and twist your wrist to wrap the bars over the top of your dominant hand, then pull back to grab the bars with both hands before landing.

NITRO METER

BEGINNER · INTERMEDIATE · ADVANCED · CRAZY!

THE FOOTPLANT

The footplant is when you take one foot off the deck of the scooter mid-trick and push that foot against an obstacle, like a ramp or wall.

Footplants are mostly done on vert ramps and ledges, making it a trick that can be performed in a park or on the streets!

NITRO METER

BEGINNER INTERMEDIATE ADVANCED CRAZY!

RIDE SAFE AND SMART!
TRICK SCOOTERING SAFETY TIPS

Being safe means more time on the scooter and less time laid up with injuries. And being safe isn't just about the right equipment—it's about riding safely, too.

To start, don't ride above your ability—especially when you're learning new tricks and techniques. Always start with and master simpler tricks before you move on to the advanced ones! You need to master the foundations to be a great rider.

PRO TIPS

NITRO CIRCUS RYAN WILLIAMS

Your scooter takes a beating when you're learning and mastering tricks. Check your wheels often for cracks and other wear. Make sure every part of your scooter is working well before you ride and that nothing is wobbly or loose!

Check the fork for any give and tighten as needed.

Make sure the deck is still sturdy and isn't starting to crack or separate from the head tube.

Check the handlebars for wear, cracks, bends, and other problems.

Be sure your wheels don't have cracks or uneven wear before you ride.

HITTING THE TRICKS AND NOTHIN' ELSE
AVOIDING HAZARDS AND HAVING FUN

When you're riding, it's important to be aware of your surroundings. Whether you're riding on the street or on ramps at a park, you need to watch out for hazards.

When you're riding on the street, you share the road with pedestrians, traffic, and even trash, glass, and other hazards. Even in a skate park, you should check the ramp for any debris and potential issues before you ride.

If you're a park rider, your most likely hazard is the other riders. Follow the basic rules and make sure the ramps are clear of riders before you drop in.

Concussions are more common in young people than in adults, and they can be cumulative, which means no matter how long it's been between a concussion, they add up to contribute to traumatic injury to your brain (which can be permanent!). Don't take any chances: ride smart and wear a good helmet.

If you're interested in learning about advanced scooter tricks, you need a specialty scooter, not a standard toy one. Don't try any of the big tricks with a toy scooter, or you will get hurt!

WHIPPING WITH STYLE
GET READY TO WHIP THAT TAIL

TRICK #7

TAILWHIP

The tailwhip is where the deck of the scooter spins around 360 degrees. Once you have a solid, consistent, and somewhat high bunny hop, you're ready to learn the tailwhip!

BEGINNER INTERMEDIATE ADVANCED CRAZY!

NITRO METER

LEARNING THE TAILWHIP!

Make sure you have a solid bunny hop down, then practice using your front foot to kick the deck around in a circle and catch it with the same foot back in place.

Separately, practice spinning the scooter in a circular motion using your wrists and forearms. It should spin around as closely as possible to your body but not hit you. You can do these steps while standing on the ground, then combine them when you're ready!

HEELWHIP

The heelwhip is basically an opposite tailwhip. It spins the opposite way, and it can be harder because it takes more effort and control to spin the deck fully around.

NITRO METER — BEGINNER, INTERMEDIATE, ADVANCED, CRAZY!

PRO TIPS

NITRO CIRCUS RYAN WILLIAMS

These are base tricks that you need to master for any trick that you do in the air. You'll be a better rider in the end!

DON'T FEAR THE 180

GIVE IT A WHIRL

THE 180

The 180 is the backbone of an almost endless supply of tricks and combos.

As you become more comfortable with your spins and have more control, you'll be ready for these more advanced tricks.

NITRO METER

BEGINNER · INTERMEDIATE · ADVANCED · CRAZY!

NITRO CIRCUS RYAN WILLIAMS

PRO TIPS

There's a big difference between frontside versus backside spinning: spinning frontside is when you spin the same way your feet are pointing (in the direction of your toes), and backside is when you spin the opposite way as your feet/footstand. Neither one is better than the other. Start with what feels more natural, then learn the harder spin later to add to your bag of tricks!

BUILDING ON THE 180
SPINNING ROUND AND ROUND

If you're getting bored with your bunny hop, practice hopping and turning (with your shoulders and head leading the way) so you're facing the opposite direction.

Start on flat ground. Once you've mastered the 180, you are halfway to a full 360!

If you've got the 180 down, you are ready to rock! It's now time to add some flair and difficulty to the 180 with some sick combos.

DID YOU KNOW?

A variation of the 180 is the half cab, also called the *fakie 180*. This trick comes from the skateboarding world, as do many of the scooter tricks you'll master. Riding fakie on a skateboard is when the back of the board is facing the direction of travel.

"The more fun you're having, **THE BETTER** you will get at riding, because if you fail with a smile on your face, then you're **NEVER DEFEATED**."

—RYAN WILLIAMS

BUILDING ON THE TAILWHIP

BE THE KING OF THE PARK

TRICK #10

DOWNWHIP

A downwhip is a tailwhip and a 180 done at the same time in opposite directions. It's easiest to learn on a slight bank or flat ground before increasing your speed and performing it with more air off a ramp.

Once you have the tailwhip dialed, this more advanced trick will take practice but will be worth the effort.

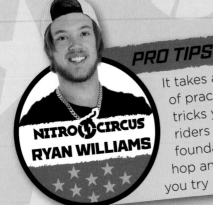

NITRO CIRCUS
RYAN WILLIAMS

PRO TIPS

It takes a long time and lots of practice to master the tricks you see top scooter riders doing. Start with the foundations, like the bunny hop and barspin, before you try the insane combos.

BEGINNER INTERMEDIATE ADVANCED CRAZY!

NITRO METER

BUILDING ON THE TAILWHIP
SCOOTERS ARE PULLING TRICKS AND TAKING NAMES!

TRICK #11

FRONT BRIFLIP

In a front briflip, the scooter flips up behind you while you let go of your outside hand (it could be either side) before grabbing the bars back down and allowing the deck to flip back beneath your feet.

This trick requires lots of speed and lots of air, but it is best to practice the movement while keeping your feet on the ground. Bringing the scooter up in front of you with both hands before snapping back down will help create the rotation needed to flip the scooter.

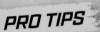

PRO TIPS

If you stand with your left foot front on the scooter (called "regular"), you'll want to spin the scooter clockwise. If you stand with your right foot in front (called "goofy"), you'll do better spinning the scooter counterclockwise. One way will feel more natural.

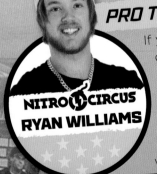

NITRO CIRCUS
RYAN WILLIAMS

NITRO METER

BEGINNER · INTERMEDIATE · ADVANCED · CRAZY!

TAILWHIP FRONT SCOOTER FLIP

A combination of a tailwhip and a front scooter flip, this intermediate-level trick will wow your friends and foes alike!

To pull off the front scooter flip whip, first get used to doing the opposite front scooter flip, which is a bit harder. Make sure you've mastered that trick before adding the whip. When you're ready, you whip the scooter and throw the front scoot at the same time. Practice this motion while on the ground first, then move to a flat surface.

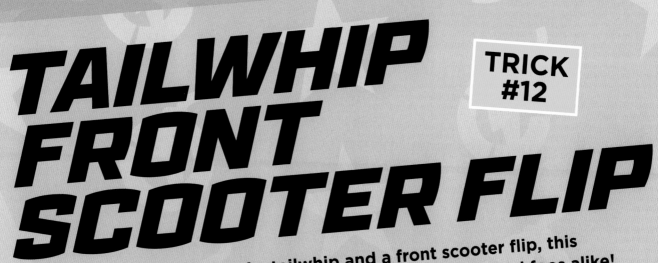

NITRO METER

BEGINNER INTERMEDIATE ADVANCED CRAZY!

WE'RE NOT DONE YET

NOTHING BUT AIR

NITRO METER
BEGINNER · INTERMEDIATE · ADVANCED · CRAZY!

TRICK #13

THE 360

Make sure you have a solid 180 down.

After that, it's simply a matter of adding momentum and power while maintaining control over the scooter and your balance. Remember to lead with your shoulders and head. Practice makes perfect! A basic 360 can be performed on flat ground before progressing to ramps.

DID YOU KNOW?

Dakota Schuetz is also the first person to land a documented 1080 on a scooter.

360 FLY-OUT

Once you have the 360 nailed, you can take it to a ramp. A fly-out means getting air off a jump or ramp.

You might find this easier than a 360 on flat ground because you will have more time to spin in the air. Plus, everything looks cooler off ramps!

CONQUERING THE RAMP!

HOW THE ███ US DO IT
KICKING AND WHIPPING

KICKLESS REWIND

A kickless is where the scooter does a ¾ tailwhip, then it's whipped back the opposite way using only your upper body—hence the name *kickless*!

It may sound simple, but it's not. Start by standing on the ground and learning the snapping movement required to bring the deck back to place after the heelwhip.

NITRO METER

BEGINNER INTERMEDIATE ADVANCED CRAZY!

PRO TIPS

You should know how to do a doublewhip and a heel rewind before you are ready for a kickless rewind! To start, practice flipping the deck back and forth while standing on the ground. Make sure you tilt your scooter to the side to stop the rotation of the tailwhip, then use your body to whip it back in the direction it came from.

NITRO CIRCUS
RYAN WILLIAMS

During the 2017 Nitro World Games Scooter Best Trick competition, Dakota Schuetz landed the world's first backflip quad kickless.

NITRO METER

BEGINNER · INTERMEDIATE · ADVANCED · CRAZY!

BACKFLIP QUAD KICKLESS

TRICK #16

ONE-FOOT GRAB

The one-foot grab is exactly what it sounds like. Once in the air, take one foot off the deck of the scooter and reach down with one hand to grab the deck.

Grab tricks can look easy, but the key to mastering them is height, not speed! Without enough air, you won't have enough time to move your hand from the handlebars to the deck and back.

BEGINNER · INTERMEDIATE · ADVANCED · CRAZY!

NITRO METER

TOBOGGAN

Grabbing the deck of your scooter during a run or jump is a great way to show off your growing skill and confidence on your scooter. Riders grab their decks to add difficulty to jumps and just to have fun and add flair to their scootering.

Off a fly-out, you tuck (you squat, really), pull your deck upward with your momentum, and grab it with one hand and hold it for a sec. Start by simply tucking, pulling, and touching your deck. Over time, you'll be able to touch for longer and longer and then finally hold it.

BEGINNER INTERMEDIATE ADVANCED CRAZY!

NITRO METER

TRICKS THAT WOW!
ADDING AN EXTRA DEGREE OF DIFFICULTY

Once you're comfortable riding, turning, and jumping, you can add difficulty to your jumps by learning some grabs. Grabs are good tricks to learn because you simply start by touching the deck, and let your skill and confidence build as you master the trick!

TRICK #18

TAILGRAB

The tailgrab involves reaching down and grabbing the back of the scooter deck with one hand.

Get some air off a ramp, then, holding the bars with one hand, squat down to grab the tail. A slight twist of the handlebars would turn a tailgrab into a toboggan!

NITRO METER
BEGINNER · INTERMEDIATE · ADVANCED · CRAZY!

TUCK NO-HANDER

Another trick from the BMX world, the tuck no-hander involves tucking your body over the handlebars and extending both arms out away from your body as far as possible and for as long as possible.

The more air you can get, the more time you will have to extend your arms and really fly!

BEGINNER INTERMEDIATE ADVANCED CRAZY!

NITRO METER

WALLRIDE

TRICK #20

Wallrides are when you, well, pop on and ride a wall (or any vertical surface). You can use wallrides to add flair to your riding, as well as change direction and momentum.

Both wheels need to be on the wall for a few seconds to be considered a legit wallride. Push your body off the wall when you're ready to pop off and continue your ride on the ground.

NITRO METER

BEGINNER · INTERMEDIATE · ADVANCED · CRAZY!

NITRO CIRCUS
RYAN WILLIAMS

PRO TIPS

Once you master the wallride, you can treat anything at the skate park like a wall and show off your skills in many combinations. You can add barspins, tailspins, and more to your wallrides to wow your adoring fans.

HANDPLANT

The handplant is a cool-looking trick, usually done at the top of a ramp. At the height of the jump, your hand briefly grabs the spine of the ramp (or the ground) while the rest of your body is heels over head! You can handplant on ramps, railings... pretty much anything you can ride up to and grab with your hand.

Like all great tricks, a good handplant is best built by starting on two feet. Stand next to a tall fence or some other stable structure and practice...jump sideways toward the fence and grab it with one hand, putting all your weight on that arm.

NITRO METER

BEGINNER INTERMEDIATE ADVANCED CRAZY!

SUPERMAN

The Superman is a fantastic trick that was adapted from the freestyle BMX world. While in the air, the rider lifts both feet off the scooter deck and pushes them back behind him, parallel to the ground, resembling Superman flying.

Push the scooter out in front of you and upward. Straighten your arms. Hang on to your scooter at all times during a Superman. It's okay if your legs don't fully extend at first—over time, you'll get better and be smashing it in no time!

SUPERMAN DECK GRAB

When you've mastered the Superman, the Superman deck grab is a little bit harder and looks even more awesome.

As you extend your legs back while doing a regular Superman, take one hand off the handlebars and grab the deck. The aim is to have both your arms and legs fully stretched with the scooter out in front of you.

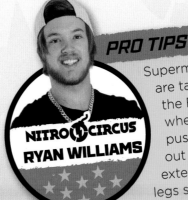

PRO TIPS

NITRO CIRCUS
RYAN WILLIAMS

Superman tricks are taken from the BMX world, where a rider pushes the bike out in front and extends his or her legs straight back.

BEGINNER · INTERMEDIATE · ADVANCED · CRAZY!

NITRO METER

BRIFLIP

This intermediate trick takes some practice. Start with the easier version, which is the front briflip.

A briflip is basically a super extended tailwhip that goes over your head! You will be flipping the scooter on the same side that your front toes are pointing, and the scooter lands where you can see it. You start by kicking the scooter out in front of you, turn the bars inward, and finish the rotation, keeping the scooter as close to your body as possible.

BEGINNER • INTERMEDIATE • ADVANCED • CRAZY!

NITRO METER

NITRO CIRCUS RYAN WILLIAMS

PRO TIPS

Start by practicing the scooter flipping motion while standing firmly on the ground. Be sure you can keep the movement consistent and the scooter close to your body.

FLAIR

The flair is a difficult trick that, once mastered, looks amazing!

The flair is a progression from a backflip where you take off from a ramp, pull back, and do a full rotation with your legs and scooter flipping over your head, to land in the same direction as you started. But the flair is done on a vert ramp or bowl, and you land in the opposite direction that you started (going back down the ramp). The key to a flair is to pull back like a backflip but drop the shoulder on the side you want to turn... This is hard!

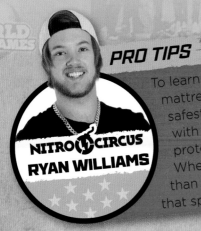

PRO TIPS

To learn flips, you need a foam pit or a mattress to begin with. The best and safest approach is to master them with a foam pit, then move to other protective surfaces, such as a resi. When you are learning flips, go faster than you normally would. You need that speed to pull off the trick.

NITRO CIRCUS RYAN WILLIAMS

NITRO METER

BEGINNER INTERMEDIATE ADVANCED CRAZY!

SKILLS THAT ADD STYLE
ADD STYLE TO AN AIR!

LOOKBACK

The lookback is a great intermediate trick many riders use to add flair to their jumps. At the height of your jump, you twist the handlebars down and to the left (if you ride left-foot forward, or "regular"), while at the same time pushing the scooter straight out to the same side of the body using your legs.

The lookback will give you confidence on your scooter, especially when jumping. It shows that you are in control and your jumps are good enough to embellish them with cool tricks.

ONE-FOOT INVERT

The one-foot invert adds pizzazz and polish to any standard jump and is a great way to build your balance and strength on your scooter. Plus, it looks cool!

When reaching the apex, or top, of your ramp jump, bring your front leg fully off and across the scooter, parallel to the ground, and then bring it back quickly to the scooter before landing. Your front foot is the foot closest to your front wheel.

NITRO METER

BEGINNER INTERMEDIATE ADVANCED CRAZY!

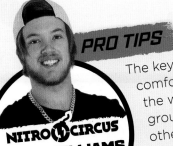

PRO TIPS

NITRO CIRCUS
RYAN WILLIAMS

The key to any trick in the air is to feel comfortable just jumping and getting the wheels of the scooter off the ground. Some tricks need more air than others, and the more air you get, the harder it is to feel comfortable, so be sure to practice getting the air you need before attempting more difficult tricks.

THE AWARD-WINNING RYAN WILLIAMS

A PIONEER IN SCOOTER RIDING

Ryan Williams, a 24-year-old from Australia, is one of the pioneers in scooter.

A Nitro Circus athlete who joined the Nitro Circus Live Tour in 2011, he has broken many records and has landed more world's first tricks than any other athlete, including the scooter triple backflip!

NITRO WORLD GAMES

At the 2017 Nitro World Games, Ryan Williams was the only athlete in the competition to make the finals in two events in two disciplines.

Williams won in Scooter Best Trick and BMX Best Trick and was the first competitor to ever win multiple events at Nitro World Games.

1st

SCOOTER BEST TRICK
JUNE 24 2017
SALT LAKE CITY, UT

RYAN
WILLIAMS

DATE OF BIRTH: June 22, 1994
HOMETOWN: Sunshine Coast, AUS

His jaw-dropping scooter tricks have changed many athletes' outlooks on scooters. One of Ryan's original tricks, the double frontflip 360, is named "Silly Willy" after him!

SILLY WILLY

"I know it may look like I land new tricks on the first try, but tricks these days take me up to 500 tries, just like it did when I first started riding! The key is to believe in yourself, and the next try could be the one you land!"

—Ryan Williams

NITRO METER

BEGINNER INTERMEDIATE ADVANCED CRAZY!

TOP SCOOTER ATHLETES PAVING THE WAY

IMPRESSIVE, ASTOUNDING, AND JUST PLAIN AMAZING!

CAPRON & COREY **FUNK**

The Funk brothers, Capron and Corey Funk, are both professional scooter athletes and social media influencers.

Adding to a long list of scooter achievements, they both podiumed at the 2016 Nitro World Games Scooter Best Trick competition, and with a joint Instagram following of more than 1.3 million, as well as 4.5 million Youtube subscribers, they are leaders in bringing scootering to the masses!

JORDAN **CLARK**

Brit Jordan Clark has been crowned world champion of scooter three years in a row!

His latest win was in June 2018 at the ISA World Finals at Imagin Extreme Barcelona championships. If that's not enough, Jordan was the first ever rider to pull off the double flair 540, an insane twisting backflip flair that many have tried but failed!

TOP SCOOTER ATHLETES PAVING THE WAY

IMPRESSIVE, ASTOUNDING, AND JUST PLAIN AMAZING!

DANTE **HUTCHINSON**

Dante Hutchinson, from East Sussex, England, is just 18 and has already won the ISA World Championship as Best Scooter Champion (in 2017).

In addition to that, he's been the UK Champion twice and came in second overall in Europe in 2015. His favorite trick is either a double inward or kickless briflip to a kick double tailwhip.

DAKOTA **SCHUETZ**

Nicknamed "The Machine," Dakota Schuetz is a 22-year-old from the United States. He's the first athlete to win every international scooter competition!

He's also a three-time ISA Scooter Competition World Champion and one of only a few riders who landed all 40 tricks of the online Tricknology challenge.

Vice President, Licensing & Publishing Amanda Joiner
Editorial Manager Carrie Bolin

Editor Jessica Firpi
Designer Luis Fuentes
Text Kezia Endsley
Proofreader Rachel Paul
Reprographics Bob Prohaska
Special Thanks to Ripley's Cartoonist, John Graziano

President Andy Edwards
Chief Commercial Officer Brett Clarke
**Vice President, Global Licensing &
  Consumer Products** Cassie Dombrowski
Vice President, Creative Dov Ribnick
Global Director, Public Relations Reid Vokey
Director, Digital Content Marketing Charley Daniels
**Global Accounts & Activation Manager,
  Consumer Products** Andrew Hogan
Art Director & Graphic Designer Joshua Geduld
Contributor Ryan Williams

Published by Ripley Publishing 2019

10 9 8 7 6 5 4 3 2 1

Copyright © 2019 Nitro Circus

ISBN: 978-1-60991-279-6

For more information regarding permission, contact:
VP Licensing & Publishing
Ripley Entertainment Inc.
7576 Kingspointe Parkway, Suite 188
Orlando, Florida 32819
Email: publishing@ripleys.com
www.ripleys.com/books

Manufactured in China in May 2019.
First Printing

Library of Congress Control Number: 2019933266

PUBLISHER'S NOTE
While every effort has been made to verify the accuracy of the entries in this book, the Publisher cannot be held responsible for any errors contained in the work. They would be glad to receive any information from readers.

WARNING
Some of the stunts and activities are undertaken by experts and should not be attempted by anyone without adequate training and supervision.

PHOTO CREDITS

2–3 (dp) Photography by Nate Christenson; **3** (tr) Photography by Sam Neill, (br) Photography by Martin Kimbell; **4–5** (dp) Photography by Chris Tedesco; **8–9** (dp) Photography by Sam Neill; **16–17** (dp) Photography by Mark Watson; **18** © travelview/Shutterstock.com; **19** © Elena Yakusheva/Shutterstock.com; **21** Photography by Sam Neill; **24–25** Photography by Martin Kimbell; **27** (tr) Photography by Sam Neill, (cr) Photography by Shelby Grimnes; **28** (t) © Andriy Blokhin/Shutterstock.com, (b) Courtesy of Ripley Cartoonist, John Graziano; **29** (sp) Photography by Martin Kimbell; **32–33** Photography by Martin Kimbell; **33** (t) © Christian Bertrand/Shutterstock.com; **35** Photography by Chris Tedesco; **36–37** (dp) © Anatoliy Karlyuk/Shutterstock.com; **38** (r) Photography by Shelby Grimnes; **40** Photography by Martin Kimbell; **41** Photography by Martin Kimbell; **46** Photography by Martin Kimbell; **49** Photography by Sam Neill; **50** Photography by Martin Kimbell; **51** (l) Photography by Sam Neill; **57** Photography by Kevin Conners; **59** Photography by Mark Watson; **60** Photography by Nate Christenson; **MASTER GRAPHICS** Nitro Meter: Created by Luis Fuentes

Special Thanks to Bell Sports, Inc., FIST Handwear PTY Ltd., Greenover Ltd.

Key: t = top, b = bottom, c = center, l = left, r = right, sp = single page, dp = double page, bkg = background

All other photos are from Nitro Circus. Every attempt has been made to acknowledge correctly and contact copyright holders, and we apologize in advance for any unintentional errors or omissions, which will be corrected in future editions.